CAROL ANN DUFFY was Poet Laureate of the United Kingdom for a decade from 2009 to 2019. Her poetry has received many awards, including the Signal Prize for Children's Verse, the Whitbread, Forward and T. S. Eliot Prizes, and the Lannan and E. M. Forster Awards in America. She won the PEN Pinter Prize in 2012, and was appointed DBE in 2015. In 2021, she was awarded the International Golden Wreath for lifetime achievement in poetry.

NATURE

Carol Ann Duffy

PICADOR

First published 2023 by Picador
an imprint of Pan Macmillan
The Smithson, 6 Briset Street, London EC1M 5NR
EU representative: Macmillan Publishers Ireland Ltd, 1st Floor,
The Liffey Trust Centre, 117–126 Sheriff Street Upper,
Dublin 1, D01 YC43
Associated companies throughout the world
www.panmacmillan.com

ISBN 978-1-5290-9694-1

1 3 5 7 9 8 6 4 2

A CIP catalogue record for this book is available from the British Library.

Printed and bound by CPI Group (UK) Ltd, Croydon, CR0 4YY

Visit *www.picador.com* to read more about all our books
and to buy them. You will also find features, author interviews and
news of any author events, and you can sign up for e-newsletters
so that you're always first to hear about our new releases.

Contents

NATURE

The Dolphins

World is what you swim in, or dance, it is simple.
We are in our element but we are not free.
Outside this world you cannot breathe for long.
The other has my shape. The other's movement
forms my thoughts. And also mine. There is a man
and there are hoops. There is a constant flowing guilt.

We have found no truth in these waters,
no explanations tremble on our flesh.
We were blessed and now we are not blessed.
After travelling such space for days we began
to translate. It was the same space. It is
the same space always and above it is the man.

And now we are no longer blessed, for the world
will not deepen to dream in. The other knows
and out of love reflects me for myself.
We see our silver skin flash by like memory
of somewhere else. There is a coloured ball
we have to balance till the man has disappeared.

The moon has disappeared. We circle well-worn grooves
of water on a single note. Music of loss forever
from the other's heart which turns my own to stone.
There is a plastic toy. There is no hope. We sink
to the limits of this pool until the whistle blows.
There is a man and our mind knows we will die here.

1985

2

A Healthy Meal

The gourmet tastes the secret dreams of cows
tossed lightly in garlic. Behind the green door, swish
of oxtails languish on an earthen dish. Here are
wishbones and pinkies; fingerbowls will absolve guilt.

Capped teeth chatter to a kidney or at the breast
of something which once flew. These hearts knew
no love and on their beds of saffron rice they lie
beyond reproach. What is the claret like? Blood.

On table six, the language of tongues is braised
in armagnac. The woman chewing suckling pig
must sleep with her husband later. Leg,
saddle and breast bleat against pure white cloth.

Alter *calf* to *veal* in four attempts. This is
the power of words; knife, tripe, lights, charcuterie.
A fat man orders his *rare* and a fine sweat
bastes his face. There are napkins to wipe the evidence

and sauces to gag the groans of abattoirs. The menu
lists the recent dead in French, from which they order
offal, poultry, fish. Meat flops in the jowls. Belch.
Death moves in the bowels. You are what you eat.

1985

4

Selling Manhattan

All yours, Injun, twenty-four bucks' worth of glass beads,
gaudy cloth. I got myself a bargain. I brandish
fire-arms and fire-water. Praise the Lord.
Now get your red ass out of here.

I wonder if the ground has anything to say.
You have made me drunk, drowned out
the world's slow truth with rapid lies.
But today I hear again and plainly see. Wherever
you have touched the earth, the earth is sore.

I wonder if the spirit of the water has anything
to say. That you will poison it. That you
can no more own the rivers and the grass than own
the air. I sing with true love for the land;
dawn chant, the song of sunset, starlight psalm.

Trust your dreams. No good will come of this.
My heart is on the ground, as when my loved one
fell back in my arms and died. I have learned
the solemn laws of joy and sorrow, in the distance
between morning's frost and firefly's flash at night.

Man who fears death, how many acres do you need
to lengthen your shadow under the endless sky?
Last time, this moment, now, a boy feels his freedom
vanish, like the salmon going mysteriously
out to sea. Loss holds the silence of great stones.

I will live in the ghost of grasshopper and buffalo.

The evening trembles and is sad.
A little shadow runs across the grass
and disappears into the darkening pines.

1987

Ape

There is a male silverback on the calendar.
Behind him the jungle is defocused,
except in one corner, where trees gargle the sun.

After you have numbered the days, you tear off
the page. His eyes hold your eyes
as you crumple a forest in your fist.

1990

The Legend

Some say it was seven tons of meat in a thick black hide
you could build a boat from, stayed close to the river
on the flipside of the sun where the giant forests were.

Had shy, old eyes. You'd need both those hands for one.
Maybe. Walked in placid herds under a jungly, sweating roof
just breathing; a dry electric wind you could hear a mile off.

Huge feet. Some say if it rained you could fish in a footprint,
fruit fell when it passed. It moved, food happened, simple.
You think of a warm, inky cave and you got its mouth all
      right.

You dream up a yard of sandpaper, damp, you're talking
      tongue.
Eat? Its own weight in a week. And water. Some say
the sweat steamed from its back in small grey clouds.

But big. Enormous. Spine like the mast on a galleon.
Ears like sails gasping for a wind. You picture
a rope you could hang a man from, you're seeing its tail.

Tusks like banisters. I almost believe myself. Can you
drum up a roar as wide as a continent, a deep hot note
that bellowed out and belonged to the melting air?
      You got it.

But people have always lied! You know some say it had
      a trunk
like a soft telescope, that it looked up along it at the sky
and balanced a bright, gone star on the end, and it died.

1990

Following Francis

Watch me. I start with a low whistle, twist it,
pitch it higher and thinner till the kestrel treads air.
There! I have a genius for this, which I offer
to God. Do they say I am crazy, brother?

Yes, they say that. My own wife said it. *Dropping*
    everything
and following that fool! You want to be covered
in birdshit? You make me sick. I left anyway,
hurried to the woods to meet him. Francis. Francis.
We had nothing. Later, I wept in his arms like a boy;
his hands were a woman's, plucking my tears off,
    tasting them.

We are animals, he said.

I am more practical. He fumbles with two sticks
hoping for fire; swears, laughs, cups glow-worms
in his palm while I start up a flame. Some nights
we've company, local accents in the dusk. He sees
my jealousy flare beneath dark trees. He knows.
I know he knows. When he looks at me, he thinks

I cannot tame this.

This evening, Francis preaches to the birds. If he is crazy,
what does that make me? I close my eyes. Tell my
    children
we move north tomorrow, away from here where the
    world
sings through cool grass, water, air, a saint's voice.
Tell them that what I am doing I do from choice.

He holds a fist to the sky and a hawk swoops down.

1990

November

How they can ruin a day, the funeral cars proceeding
over the edge of the Common, while fat black crows
leer and jeer in gangs. A parliament all right.

Suddenly the hour is less pleasant than it first appeared
to take a walk and post a harmless, optimistic letter.
Face up to it. It is far too hot for November

and far too late for more than the corpse stopped
at a red light near the Post Office, where you pause
wishing you could make some kind of gesture

like the old woman who crosses herself as the hearse
 moves on.

1990

River

At the turn of the river the language changes,
a different babble, even a different name
for the same river. Water crosses the border,
translates itself, but words stumble, fall back,
and there, nailed to a tree, is proof. A sign

in new language brash on a tree. A bird,
not seen before, singing on a branch. A woman
on the path by the river, repeating a strange sound
to clue the bird's song and ask for its name, after.
She kneels for a red flower, picks it, later
will press it carefully between the pages of a book.

What would it mean to you if you could be
with her there, dangling your own hands in the water
where blue and silver fish dart away over stone,
stoon, stein, like the meanings of things, vanish?
She feels she is somewhere else, intensely, simply because
of words; sings loudly in nonsense, smiling, smiling.

If you were really there what would you write on a postcard,
or on the sand, near where the river runs into the sea?

1990

Demeter

Where I lived — winter and hard earth.
I sat in my cold stone room
choosing tough words, granite, flint,

to break the ice. My broken heart —
I tried that, but it skimmed,
flat, over the frozen lake.

She came from a long, long way,
but I saw her at last, walking,
my daughter, my girl, across the fields,

in bare feet, bringing all spring's flowers
to her mother's house. I swear
the air softened and warmed as she moved,

the blue sky smiling, none too soon,
with the small shy mouth of a new moon.

1999

The Virgin's Memo

maybe not abscesses, acne, asthma,
son, maybe not boils,
maybe not cancer
or diarrhoea
or tinnitus of the inner ear,
maybe not fungus,
maybe rethink the giraffe,
maybe not herpes, son,
or (text illegible)
or jellyfish
or (untranslatable)
maybe not leprosy or lice,
the menopause or mice, mucus, son,
neuralgia, nits,
maybe not body odour,
piles,
quicksand, quagmires,
maybe not rats, son, rabies, rattlesnakes,
shite,
and maybe hang fire on the tarantula,
the unicorn's lovely,
but maybe not veruccas

or wasps,
or (text illegible)
or (untranslatable)
maybe not . . .

2002

Haworth

I'm here now where you were.
The summer grass under my palms is your hair.
Your taste is the living air.

I lie on my back. Two juggling butterflies are your smile.
The heathery breath of the moor's simply your smell.
Your name sounds on the coded voice of the bell.

I'll go nowhere you've not.
The bleached dip in a creature's bone's your throat.
That high lark, whatever it was you thought.

And this ridged stone your hand in mine,
and the curve of the turning earth your spine,
and the swooning bees besotted with flowers your tune.

I get up and walk. The dozing hillside is your dreaming
head.
The cobblestones are every word you said.
The grave I kneel beside, only your bed.

2005

Spring

Spring's pardon comes, a sweetening of the air,
the light made fairer by an hour, time
as forgiveness, granted in the murmured colouring
of flowers, rain's mantra of reprieve, reprieve, reprieve.

The lovers waking in the lightening rooms believe
that something holds them, as they hold themselves,
within a kind of grace, a soft embrace, an absolution
from their stolen hours, their necessary lies. And this is
      wise:

to know that music's gold is carried in the frayed purse
of a bird, to pick affection's herb, to see the sun and moon
half-rhyme their light across the vacant, papery sky.
Trees, in their blossoms, young queens, flounce for
      clemency.

2005

18

Ariel

Where the bee sucks,
neonicotinoid insecticides
in a cowslip's bell lie,
in fields purple with lavender,
yellow with rape,
and on the sunflower's upturned face;
on land monotonous with cereals and grain,
merrily,
      merrily;
sour in the soil,
sheathing the seed, systemic
in the plants and crops,
the million acres to be ploughed,
seething in the orchards now,
under the blossom
          that hangs
on the bough.

2011

Virgil's Bees

Bless air's gift of sweetness, honey
from the bees, inspired by clover,
marigold, eucalyptus, thyme,
the hundred perfumes of the wind.
Bless the beekeeper

                    who chooses for her hives
a site near water, violet beds, no yew,
no echo. Let the light lilt, leak, green
or gold, pigment for queens,
and joy be inexplicable but *there*
in harmony of willowherb and stream,
of summer heat and breeze,

                        each bee's body
at its brilliant flower, lover-stunned,
strumming on fragrance, smitten.

                         For this,
let gardens grow, where beelines end,
sighing in roses, saffron blooms, buddleia;
where bees pray on their knees, sing, praise
in pear trees, plum trees; bees
are the batteries of orchards, gardens, guard them.

2011

Atlas

Give him strength, crouched on one knee in the dark
with the Earth on his back,

                      balancing the seven seas,
the oceans, five, kneeling
in ruthless, empty, endless space

                        for grace
of whale, dolphin, sea-lion, shark, seal, fish, every kind
which swarms the waters. Hero.

                    Hard, too,
heavy to hold, the mountains;
burn of his neck and arms taking the strain –
Andes, Himalayas, Kilimanjaro –
give him strength, he heaves them high
to harvest rain from skies for streams
and rivers, he holds the rivers,
holds the Amazon, Ganges, Nile, hero, hero.

Hired by no one, heard in a myth only, lonely,
he carries a planet's weight,
                                    islands and continents,
the billions there, his ears the last to hear
their language, music, gunfire, prayer;
give him strength, strong girth, for elephants,
tigers, snow leopards, polar bears, bees, bats,
the last ounce of a hummingbird.

                              Broad-backed
in infinite, bleak black,
                        he bears where Earth is, nowhere,
head bowed, a genuflection to the shouldered dead,
the unborn's hero, he is love's lift;
sometimes the moon rolled to his feet, given.

2011

Hive

All day we leave and arrive at the hive,
concelebrants. The hive is love,
what we serve, preserve, avowed in Latin murmurs
as we come and go, skydive, freighted
with light, to where we thrive, us, in time's hum,
on history's breath,
                                        industrious, identical . . .

there suck we,
alchemical, nectar-slurred, pollen-furred,
the world's mantra us, our blurry sound
along the thousand scented miles to the hive,
haven, where we unpack our foragers;
or heaven-stare, drone-eyed, for a queen's star;
or nurse or build in milky, waxy caves,
the hive, alive, us – how we behave.

2011

Nile

When I went, wet, wide, white and blue, my name Nile,
you'd kneel near to net fish, or would wade
where I shallowed, or swim in my element,
or sing a lament for the child drowned where I was too
    deep,
too fast; but once you found, in my reeds,
a boy in a basket.
                I gushed, fresh lake, salt sea,
utterly me, source to mouth, without me, drought,
    nought,
for my silt civilized –
                      from my silt, pyramids.
Where I went, undammed, talented,
food, wine, work, craft, art;
no Nile, nil, null, void.
                  I poured, full spate, roared,
voiced water, calling you in from dust, thirst, burn,
to where you flourished; Pharaoh, firstborn . . .
now Cleopatra's faint taste still on my old tongue.

2011

The English Elms

Seven Sisters in Tottenham,
long gone, except for their names,
were English elms.

Others stood at the edge of farms,
twinned with the shapes of clouds
like green rhymes;
or cupped the beads of rain
in their leaf palms;
or glowered, grim giants, warning of storms.

In the hedgerows in old films,
elegiacally, they loom,
the English elms;
or find posthumous fame
in the lines of poems –
the music making elm –
for ours is a world without them . . .

to whom the artists came,
time upon time,
scumbling, paint on their fingers and thumbs;
and the woodcutters, who knew the elm
was a coffin's deadly aim;
and the mavis, her filled nest unharmed
in the crook of a living, wooden arm;
and boys, with ball, bat, stumps
for a game;
and nursing ewes and lambs, calm
under English elms . . .

great, masterpiece trees
who were overwhelmed.

2011

Luke Howard, Namer of Clouds

Eldezar and Asama Yama, 1783,
erupted violently; a *Great Fogg*
blending incredible skies over Europe.
In London, Luke Howard was ten.
The sky's lad then.

               Smitten,
he stared up evermore; saw
a meteor's fiery spurt,
the clamouring stars;
what the moon wouldn't do;
but loved clouds most —
dragons and unicorns;
Hamlet's camels, weasels and whales;
the heads of heroes;
the sword of Excalibur, lit
by the setting sun.
               Mackerel sky,
mackerel sky, not long wet,
not long dry.

And knew
love goes naming,
even a curl of hair — thus, Cirrus.
Cumulus. Stratus. Nimbus.

2011

The Woman in the Moon

Darlings, I write to you from the moon
where I hide behind famous light.
How could you think it ever a man up here?
A cow jumped over. The dish ran away with

the spoon. What reached me were your joys, griefs,
here's-the-craic, losses, longings, your lives
brief, mine long, a talented loneliness. I must have
a thousand names for the earth, my blue vocation.

Round I go, the moon a diet of light, sliver of pear,
wedge of lemon, slice of melon, half an orange,
silver onion; your human sound falling through space,
childbirth's song, the lover's song, the song of death.

Devoted as words to things, I gaze, gawp, glare; deserts
where forests were, sick seas. When night comes,
I see you gaping back as though you hear my *Darlings,
what have you done, what have you done to the world?*

2011

Parliament

Then in the writers' wood,
every bird with a name in the world
crowded the leafless trees,
took its turn to whistle or croak.
An owl grieved in an oak.
A magpie mocked. A rook
cursed from a sycamore.
The cormorant spoke:

Stinking seas
below ill winds. Nothing swims.
A vast plastic soup, thousand miles
wide as long, of petroleum crap.

A bird of paradise wept in a willow.
The jewel of a hummingbird shrilled
on the air.
A stork shawled itself like a widow.
The gull said:
Where coral was red, now white, dead
under stunned waters.
The language of fish
cut out at the root.

Mute oceans. Oil like a gag
on the Gulf of Mexico.

A woodpecker heckled.
A vulture picked at its own breast.
Thrice from the cockerel, as ever.
The macaw squawked:
                              Nouns I know —
Rain. Forest. Fire. Ash.
Chainsaw. Cattle. Cocaine. Cash.
Squatters. Ranchers. Loggers. Looters.
Barons. Shooters.

A hawk swore.
A nightingale opened its throat
in a garbled quote.
A worm turned in the blackbird's beak.
This from the crane:
What I saw — slow thaw
in permafrost; broken terrain
of mud and lakes;
peat broth; seepage; melt;
methane breath.

A bat hung like a suicide.
Only a rasp of wings from the raven.
A heron was stone; a robin blood
in the written wood.
So snow and darkness slowly fell;
the eagle, history, in silhouette,
with the golden plover,
and the albatross
                    telling of Arctic ice
as the cold, hard moon calved from the earth.

2011

A Rare Bee

I heard tell of a tale of a rare bee,
kept in a hive in a forest's soul
by a hermit – hairshirt, heart long hurt –
and that this bee made honey so pure,
when pressed to the pout of a poet
it made her profound; or if smeared
on the smile of a singer it sweetened his sound;
or when eased on the eyes of an artist,
Pablo Picasso lived and breathed;
                              so I saddled my steed.

No birds sang in the branches over my head,
though I saw the wreaths of empty nests
on the ground as I rode – girl, poet, knight –
deeper into the trees, where the white hart
was less than a ghost or a thought, was light
as the written word; legend. But what wasn't going, gone,
I mused, from the land, or the sky, or the sea?
I dismounted my bony horse to walk;
out of the silence, I fancied I heard
                              the bronze buzz of a bee.

So I came to kneel at the hermit's hive —
a little church, a tiny mosque — in a mute glade
where the loner mouthed and prayed, blind
as the sun, and saw with my own eyes
one bee dance alone on the air.
I uttered my prayer: *Give me your honey,*
bless my tongue with rhyme, poetry, song.
It flew at my mouth and stung.
Then the terrible tune of the hermit's grief.
Then a gesturing, dying bee

      on the bier of a leaf.

2011

The Human Bee

I became a human bee at twelve,
when they gave me my small wand,
my flask of pollen,
and I walked with the other bees
out to the orchards.

I worked first in apples,
                              climbed the ladder
into the childless arms of a tree
and busied myself, dipping and tickling,
 duping and tackling, tracing
the petal's guidelines
down to the stigma.
                              Human, humming,
I knew my lessons by heart:
the ovary would become the fruit,
the ovule the seed,
fertilized by my golden touch, my Midas dust.

I moved to lemons,
                              head and shoulders
lost in blossom; dawn till dusk,
my delicate blessing.
All must be docile, kind, unfraught
for one fruit —
                              pomegranate, lychee,
nectarine, peach, the rhymeless orange.
And if an opening bud
                              was out of range,
I'd jump from my ladder onto a branch
and reach.

So that was my working life as a bee,
till my eyesight blurred,
my hand was a trembling bird
                              in the leaves,
the bones of my fingers thinner than wands.

And when they retired me,
I had my wine from the silent vines,
and I'd known love,
and I'd saved some money —

but I could not fly and I made no honey.

2011

Lessons in the Orchard

An apple's soft thump on the grass, somewhen
in this place. What was it? Beauty of Bath.
What was it? Yellow, vermillion, round, big, splendid;
already escaping the edge of itself,

                              like the mantra of bees,
like the notes of rosemary, tarragon, thyme.
Poppies scumble their colour onto the air,
now and there, here, then and again.

                         Alive-alive-oh,
the heart's impulse to cherish; thus,
a woman petalling paint onto a plate –
cornflower blue –
as the years pressed out her own violet ghost;
that slow brush of vanishing cloud on the sky.

And the dragonfly's talent for turquoise.
And the goldfish art of the pond.
And the open windows calling the garden in.

This bowl, life, that we fill and fill.

2014

Elephants

When I was small, I saw the circus elephants
on Blackpool sands;
a slow line of extraordinary sadness.
An elephant holds more anguish than a man.

We should not see them, except
where they choose to be,
in their grey empathies, their bulked knowledge.
They walk on song; gravity's grave clergy.

They are perfect for the earth,
its emigrant distances, its pooled waters.
If the gods were to gaze at this world,
they would hazard elephants.

2018

Treasure Beach

I wrote hard up against the sea,
which was having none of it;
more trying to name a new cloud
than looking at the verb-mad waves,
when the sea

        conjured a dolphin.

There was no one to tell;
only my lonely shout
to pitch all I held of delight, or grief,
as the dolphin leapt in staves

            over the water.

Oh Oh Oh.
The world will shake us off for what we have done
and the sea have the last word.

2018

Blackbird

And when I twitched the crisp, white cloth from the tray
to reveal my slice of the King's pie, a blackbird,
cauled in pastry, sang on the plate; an olive
anchored its tiny foot to the dainty dish.

The yellow halo of its eye was a ring
to marry song; its golden beak, a nib
to write on days . . . but as I put my knife and fork
to its breast, its wings opened; like it prayed.

All day and night, I fasted, till the bird,
peculiarly the music of God, slept;
then I pounced, feasted — a disgrace of feathers
on the floor — pouring the King's fine wine.

Now I have its whistle on my mulchy breath;
a spill of little bones boiled in a broth.

2018

Io

She could bear the force
that bent her on all fours;
her eyes splaying to soft fruits;
hands, feet, chiselled to hooves;
and the useless vowel of her voice
and the ceaseless, vile flies.

But this was not yet Hell.
That was the birthing stall
where they stole her calf
and her pumped milk was industrial grief;
where they soon returned, returned
with their needles of sperm.

The Gods who did with her as they pleased;
the meat-eaters, the lovers of cheese.

2018

Shakespeare in His Garden

Fame kicked off like boots after a long trek
and his lame foot cooling on the grass.

Ale from the pocked maid with the eye
who skittered sideways, glancing, shy.

Back to the mulberry tree, he thought naught
but went naming, in his boy-manner . . .

aloe, bee, columbine, daisy, eglantine . . .
till his soul rhymed with his senses.

His father's reek in the ale. His mother's scent
in the thyme thumbed to dust on his palm.

The tall sun stooped to chrism his head.
The church-bell told the hour his name.

Then four butterflies like stifled mirth;
a slow heartbeat of apples falling.

Beyond the warm walls, all Warwickshire;
willows, ashes, a thousand elms, collaborators;

like the backstage dovecote, the full-house beehive.
Poetry a stale marriage now. He tried to care.

Cared not. And the knot-garden laced, unlaced,
its several fragrances . . . *hot lavender, mints, marjoram.*

So he listed: but the words were loose beads, no necklace.
The breath of flowers far sweeter in the air than in the
      hand.

2018

The Creation of Adam and Eve

*(from the York Pageant of the Cardmakers,
15th Century)*

In heaven and earth, in space, place,
my five days graft ends
with more than there was, with plus;
so I think it time well spent.

Heaven has stars, planets, bright
in their courses to move.
The moon is servant to night.
The sun is first love.

Earth has true trees, grass grace;
beasts and birds, brided, great and small,
fishes in flood, insects, snakes,
live, thrive, and have my blessing, all.

World work wrought now at my will.
I look and listen, hear no praise
from beasts without reason or skill
to honour this, me, maker of days.

So I will form a new beast, best,
to husband the fair world;
after my shape and likeness,
worshipful, rational, good child.

I make man now from plain earth;
for him to have in mind
how simple he is at birth
he will be at the end; all humankind.

Stand up, earth, in blood and bone
with the body of man, seize life.
I will not have him live alone;
from his left rib cleave a wife.

Both receive your souls from me,
the ghost of being, breathe,
be skilful. Your names shall be
Adam and Eve. Love.

2018

Ferns

I cut back the brittle fronds
and there are the seven crosiers,
praying in a circle;
their rough, brown habits hooded,
though it is light they solicit,
under the canopy of beech and sycamore;
beyond, a listening heaven.

2018

Forest

In fact, the trees are murmuring under your feet,
a buried empathy, you tread it.

                              High over your head,
the canopy learns light; a conversation
you lip-read. The forest

                            keeps different time;
slow hours as long as your life,
so you feel human.

So you feel more human; persuaded what you are
by wordless breath of wood, reason in resin.
You might name them –

                        oak, ash, holly, beech –
but the giants are silence alive, superior,
and now you are all instinct;
swinging the small lamp of your heart
as you venture their world:

the green, shadowy, garlic air

                                            your ancestors breathed.

Ah, you thought love human
till you lost yourself in the forest,
but it is more strange.

                                           These grave and patient saints

who pray and pray
and suffer your little embrace.

2019

Will

I have spent my time
depositing my eyesight
on the moon. Behold
your inheritance.

2020

Nest

I was a mother again, when you came back
from the broken world; to wait with me
for our garden to wake from its cold sleep,
while scientists stirred and sipped at their vaccines.

In the winter of lockdown year, you cut your own hair;
placing the pale brown tresses and locks
on newspaper. *May I have?* I said.

I'd read somewhere that birds would use hair
for their nests; so when the snowdrops came and went,
I put it down on the softening grass —
bronze and copper and gold on green.

Then I snipped it safe; left it there
for the rain to rinse, for the sun to dry.
By spring, it was gone. I saw a wren
with a beakful of moss; a blackbird tug at a web.

You laughed when I told. *What the actual . . . ?*
But I am your mother and when you leave,
I will not see, or search for, the nests I know
to be there. In every one, a strand of your hair.

2021

When

The weight of the world
fell on the frail shoulders of words,
you applied for the post of under-gardener
in your own garden.

Your first task was to dig a hole.
You set to; watched by the wooden eyes
of the hawthorn trees;
the difference between you, time.

So, a pond. You lowered the lilies
into their liquid grave.
All that rhymed with your hand,
your other hand.

It was a year and a day,
before you saw the Green Man's face
in a tangle of branches and leaves;
breathing his green breath.

But by then you had learned
to be slow. An unbothering,
you might have said, had you
been bothered.

The wind blew through
the Green Man's mouth.
His lips moved; uttering
something and nothing; unpublished.

But the mistle-thrush
spread its wings in the soil,
an open book;
the bees at their grammar.

Once, the light and the moment
clicked like a code
and the place was sentient —
like a falling in love.

And then like a failing in love.

2022